I0831074

THE PERFECT PET!

whitestar kids

CONTENTS

CATS

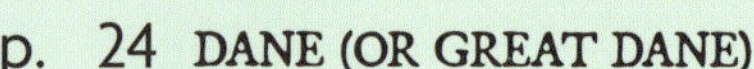

DOGS

RODENTS

FINS, SCALES, AND FEATHERS

FRIENDS FROM ALL OVER THE WORLD!

WHAT IS THE PERFECT PET FOR YOU?

CATS

Small, fluffy ninjas with a degree in naps

They are said to have nine lives, and black ones bring bad luck. Well, yes: cats are such widespread animals that they have centuries of legends behind them! They are among the absolute most beloved pets in the whole world. And many breeds are named after where they are from.

Let's discover some of them together!

SIAMESE

These cats have enchanting blue eyes and a slender, tapered body that is very elegant. The breed comes from Siam, the ancient name for present-day Thailand, and it is said that these cats were used as guards of sacred temples.

Today, Siamese cats are spread all over the world, but they are always very recognizable thanks to their magnificent light fur, which becomes darker on paws, muzzle, tail, and ears!

They are extremely playful and athletic cats, and they need to be entertained for a long time. Siamese cats can live up to 15 years!

CAT FACTS

Siamese cats are great talkers: they love their family and "tell them" every chance they get!

Intelligence ●●●●
Playfulness ●●●●●
Lovingness ●●●

EUROPEAN

The European cat is certainly among the most popular and beloved breeds: it is the tiger cat par excellence!

Various studies claim that it is a direct descendant of the ancient Egyptian cat that was revered as a deity.

Its body is strong and agile: it can be seen in action with quick jumps and runs both indoors and outdoors. Better to have a home fit for...an athlete!

DID YOU KNOW?

Nine lives like a cat? That is an urban legend that has no underlying truth! Our cats, like all animals, have only one life, so we must take care of them as best as possible.

Intelligence

Playfulness

Lovingness

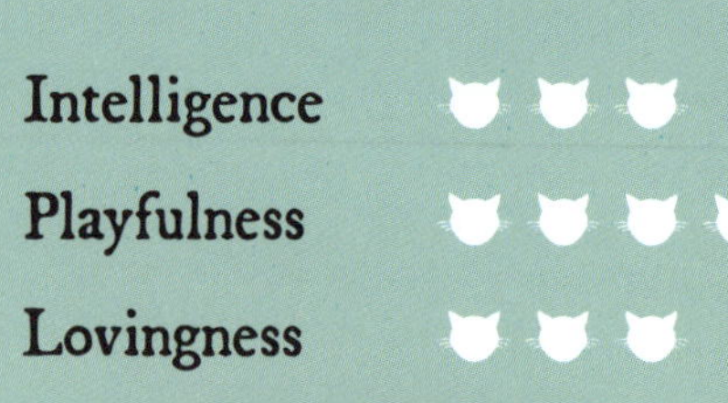

MESTIZO

This cat doesn't belong to one breed—it's quite a mix! These cats are the ones most often seen on the streets and in feline colonies.

You can find them in all coat colors and can adopt one from your local kennel. For the most part, they are very cuddly animals and attached to the family in which they live: get ready for some marathon scratching sessions!

Mixed-breed cats live longer than purebred cats.

DID YOU KNOW?

Cats are real sleepyheads—they can snooze for up to 18 hours a day!

PERSIAN

Intelligence 🐱🐱🐱🐱
Playfulness 🐱🐱
Lovingness 🐱🐱🐱

Fluffy, thick fur, flattened muzzle, and magnetic eyes—that's the Persian cat! It loves to be with its family, but beware, it doesn't adapt very well to change.

Best not to adopt it if you move or travel often, as it may show you all its annoyance!

Often, the breed name tells us the origin, but not in this case! The very furry Persian comes from England, not Persia, the ancient name for Iran.

CAT FACTS

A perfect way to entertain your feline friend? Get a simple cardboard box it can fit into—it'll immediately flop into it with great satisfaction!

CARTHUSIAN

This is a magnificent cat with distinctive gray fur.

Its body is muscular and it loves to play, yet it is usually of an affectionate and quiet disposition. It certainly appreciates a scratching post or a ball to chase between rooms to let loose every now and then!

Apparently, the breed was named after a French monastery where these cats were said to be bred!

Intelligence 4/4
Playfulness 3/4
Lovingness 4/4

CAT FACTS

When they see themselves in the mirror, cats don't recognize themselves!

ABYSSINIAN

With its deep eyes, big ears, and elegant gait, this cat has been enchanting for centuries! Apparently, in fact, its origins are very ancient.

Today, it can be found in many homes, where it demonstrates all its energy by playing to its heart's content and letting itself be cuddled by family members to whom it particularly attaches. If you love to have caress marathons, this is the kitty for you!

This cat does not like to be alone: if you decide to adopt it, be prepared to give it lots of attention!

DID YOU KNOW?

When did cats start living with humans? Based on archaeological discoveries, about 5,000 years ago in China!

Intelligence

Playfulness 

Lovingness 

Intelligence
Playfulness
Lovingness

SIBERIAN

This breed originated from the forests of Siberia, where it lived freely for decades before being domesticated by humans. This is one of the reasons why it is a strong, stocky animal with a thick, fluffy coat.

Agile and athletic, it is perfect for those who do not like to sit still! It is very friendly and affectionate with both humans and other pets in the house.

In Russia, the Siberian cat is traditionally considered a good luck charm and a keeper of monasteries.

DID YOU KNOW?

Cats can make very different sounds—as many as a hundred have been counted!

ANGORA

Intelligence
Playfulness
Lovingness

This feline has a silky coat, and stroking it is incredible! But you should not fool yourself: although it is very affectionate, the Angora cat is a strong and active animal, as well as extremely intelligent.

If you choose to adopt it, you must prepare to entertain it with games and pastimes. It needs space to run around, both inside and outside the house!

In Turkey, the place where the breed originated, they are called "cats of desire." It is said that by whispering a wish in this animal's ear, it will come true!

CAT FACTS

When relaxed, cats purr—be careful, though, they also purr in uncomfortable situations!

CORNISH REX

Lean, tapered body and large, pointed ears—this breed is unmistakable! Straight from Cornwall, a coastal area of the United Kingdom, comes this magnificent cat who loves to live in families. That's right: it bonds very much with its adopters and follows them everywhere!

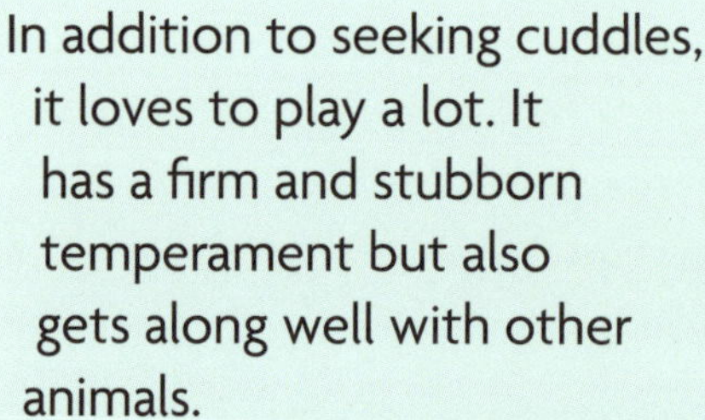

In addition to seeking cuddles, it loves to play a lot. It has a firm and stubborn temperament but also gets along well with other animals.

This cat loves the heat, but beware of the sun: it gets sunburned easily!

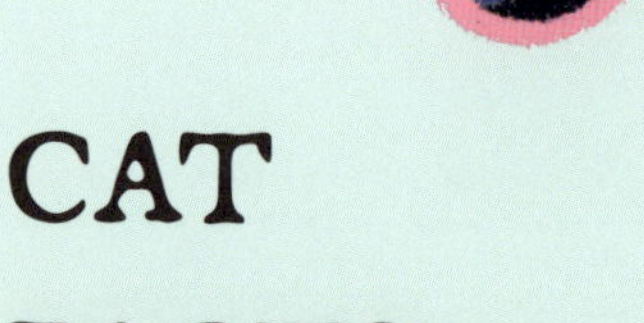

CAT FACTS

What is the maximum running speed of a domestic cat? Thirty miles per hour—not bad!

Intelligence

Playfulness

Lovingness

CEYLON

Also known as the "forest cat of Sri Lanka," the place (formerly called Ceylon) from which the breed originated, this medium-small animal is a true guardian of the home.

In fact, one of its main characteristics is that it is extremely territorial and attached to its family.

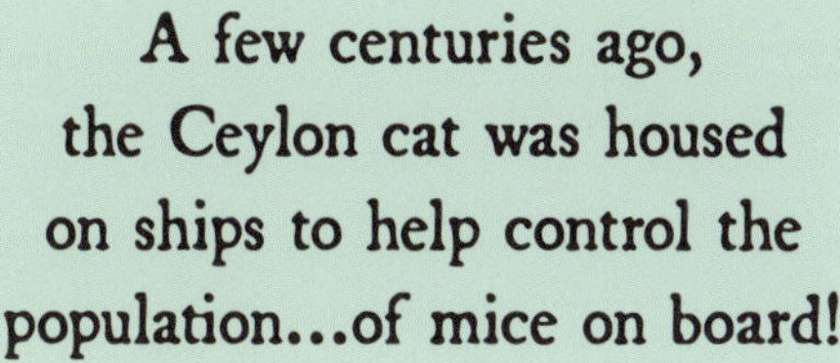

A few centuries ago, the Ceylon cat was housed on ships to help control the population...of mice on board!

DID YOU KNOW?

Cats are great jumpers: they can leap six times their length!

Intelligence

Playfulness

Lovingness

Intelligence ♥♥♥

Playfulness ♥♥

Lovingness ♥♥♥

BURMESE

Those who love cats with thick, fluffy fur cannot resist this breed. It has deep blue eyes and extremities, as well as muzzle, that are darker than the light coat. A real beauty!

If you adopt it, you will soon see it following family members, and even other pets, all over the house—it is so affectionate that it never wants to be alone! It likes to play, but it does not romp easily: it prefers cuddles!

The Burmese cat is a cross between the Siamese and Persian cats.

DID YOU KNOW?

What animal is the ancestor of the cat? The tiger!

MAINE COON

Intelligence
Playfulness
Lovingness

Has anyone asked for a maxi cat? Well, here it is! Specimens of this breed can measure up to 1 meter in length. And that's not their only record: they also have more fingers than other cats.

They are also great climbers: if you don't have an outdoor space for them to play in, it's best to provide structures for them to enjoy.

Unlike other breeds, these cats are not afraid of water!

CAT FACTS

The longest living cat died at over 38 years old!

RAGDOLL

It may well be said that the characteristics of this breed are tameness, sweetness, and... a passion for cuddles!

It is a large animal with thick and very soft fur, for which great care must be taken: better to avoid boring hairballs!

The breed appeared in the 1960s in California. It all began in the home of Ann Baker, who, wanting to create a large, long-haired cat with a sweet temperament, chose some particularly hairy neighborhood cats as companions for her affectionate white cat, Josephine!

CAT FACTS

How do cats walk? They lay their right paws first, then their left paws.

Intelligence

Playfulness

Lovingness

ORIENTAL SHORT-HAIRED

You can recognize it at first glance: triangular muzzle, large pointed ears, and elongated green eyes. The fur—well, its name says it—is super short and soft! When adopted, it immediately bonds with family members, whom it loves to cuddle with.

Active and athletic, it always wants to play and is known for its curiosity: in the house you need to be very careful, as it is capable of sneaking everywhere, especially where it shouldn't!

This cat hates being left alone: best not to adopt it if you spend little time in the house!

DID YOU KNOW?

When a cat narrows his eyes, what does it mean? He is very relaxed!

Intelligence

Playfulness

Lovingness

FOUR PURRFECTLY PECULIAR CATS

MANX

Isle of Man cats, also known as "Manx," have a feature that makes them unique: they have no tail! This is due to a genetic mutation. They have round bodies and thick fur, which can be found in any color. They are playful and very long-lived: many of them spend more than 20 years with their family!

Intelligence
Playfulness
Lovingness

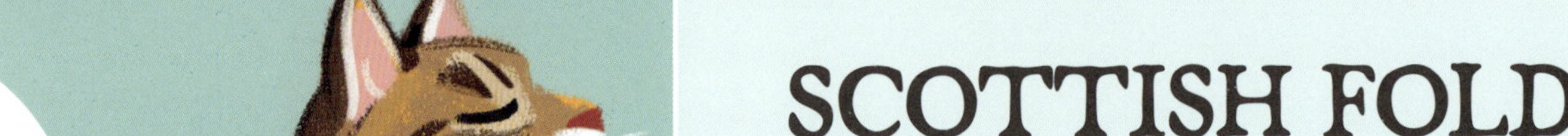

Intelligence
Playfulness
Lovingness

SCOTTISH FOLD

This breed of Scottish origin has one thing that sets it apart: the tiny ears folded forward! You cannot escape emitting an "Ohhhh!" when you see one! It not only looks very sweet but also has a mild and very affectionate nature. And it can communicate very well with its behavior! In a short time, you can tell what it means by its meows, purrs, and way of rubbing against your legs!

NORWEGIAN

This breed comes from the North. Like all forest cats, it has a strong, robust body with thick, soft fur suitable for harsh climates. It has a very independent character, but this does not prevent it from becoming attached to its adopters.
It loves to play and especially to explore: it is perfect for those who live in a home with a garden where it can venture out safely. However, its wild side, as a true hunter, often leaves room for affectionate moments with its family members.

Intelligence
Playfulness
Lovingness

Intelligence
Playfulness
Lovingness

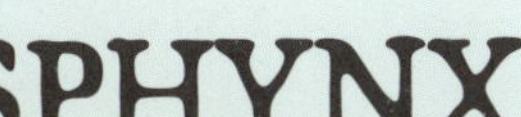

SPHYNX

Beware, naked cat in sight! That's right: this very special breed is known for its total lack of fur! Its skin color ranges from a classic pink tone to darker gray or black, and it feels incredible to the touch! It has a sweet and playful nature, and is extremely affectionate with its family. Due to the absence of a coat, it is necessary to care for it carefully: for example, its nails must always be short so that it does not injure itself.

DOGS

Four-legged wagging happiness

Who is man's best friend? The dog! This is what tradition tells us, which is based, however, on a historical truth. All dogs are descended from gray wolves, who, thousands of years ago, were domesticated by man until they became their faithful companions. There are dozens of breeds in the world today: small and very, very large dogs, furry or hairless...

...in short, a real canine universe to immerse yourself in!

Intelligence 4/5
Playfulness 3/5
Lovingness 4/5

DANE (OR GREAT DANE)

Is anyone intimidated by large dogs? The members of this breed really are large, and if they stand up on their hind legs they can surpass in height many grown men! But they are "good giants": despite their size, they are sweet, tame, and very affectionate.

To adopt one, however, it is necessary to have a large home, possibly with an outdoor space. And keep in mind to give it a lot of exercise, going for walks with it—you'll get some great muscles out of it!

Centuries ago, this breed was used for hunting wild boar in Germany, its country of origin.

DID YOU KNOW?

A Dane became the main character in a very famous cartoon: Scooby Doo!

MESTIZO

Intelligence
Playfulness
Lovingness

Precise descriptions cannot be given of these dogs because they are found in all sizes and colors!

They do not belong to a precise breed and are born from many crosses, so they have various characteristics, but for this very reason one thing is certain: every half-breed is a dog absolutely unique in the world!

The half-breed is also called a "hybrid dog" because it is born from a crossbreed of different breeds.

WOOF-WOW!

Are dogs able to dream? According to scientific research, yes! When their sleep enters the REM phase, their brain activity increases.

Intelligence
Playfulness
Lovingness

The dachshund, often called a "wiener dog" due to its long body and short legs, is a small but spirited breed.

DACHSHUND

Originally bred in Germany for hunting small game like badgers, dachshunds are known for their courage, curiosity, and tenacity. Despite their small statue, they have big personalities and are often playful!

WOOF-WOW!

Dogs are endowed with what is called a "biological clock"—they can tell when it is time for meals, walks, and play.

CHIHUAHUA

The name of this breed evokes a small, helpless-looking creature, but beware: centuries ago in Central America, where it originated, the Chihuahua was considered a sacred animal by pre-Columbian peoples.

These animals are among the smallest of dog breeds, but they have character to spare! They are ready to defend their family members, to whom they become very attached, and they do so by barking and showing their tiny—yet pointed—teeth!

This is one of the longest-lived breeds in the world, and some Chihuahuas are known to have reached 20 years of life!

DID YOU KNOW?

The smallest dog? The Chihuahua! And the largest? The Dane! The fastest one? The Greyhound! The heaviest? The Saint Bernard!

Intelligence
Playfulness
Lovingness

BICHON FRISÉ

It is very difficult to resist a dog so...fluffy! Small in size and with a very soft white coat, the bichon frisé is a sweet and lively dog. It is a sociable animal and suitable for apartment living, even in the presence of other animals.

The only important thing for this breed is to be with the family it lives with, and it is a great playful dog: at home and outside it is often seen running, jumping, and wagging its tail, trying to win over even strangers with its cheerfulness!

These little dogs suffer from severe lacrimation, which dyes the fur around their eyes a reddish color.

DID YOU KNOW?

Here's a useful tip: If you have to leave a dog alone for a few hours, you can give it a piece of clothing, so that the animal can calm down by smelling one of the family members.

Intelligence ✓✓✓

Playfulness ✓✓✓✓

Lovingness ✓✓✓✓

PEKINGESE

This dog with a funny flattened muzzle and thick fur comes from the East and is the ultimate "lap dog"! Although it is lively and playful, it likes a quiet life and hates loud noises.

Friendly with those it knows, it is wary of strangers, although it is not aggressive at all.
Its health is delicate, and it needs a lot of care and attention.

For centuries, dogs of this breed were bred in Chinese imperial palaces, where they were held in the highest esteem.

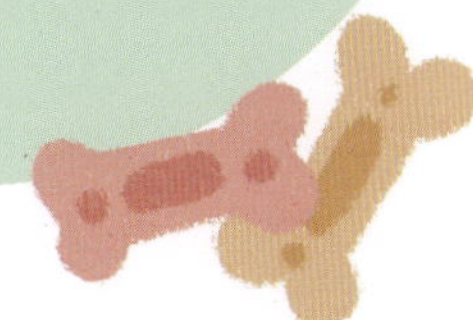

WOOF-WOW!

Dogs don't sweat like we do! They only sweat on their paws and maintain a constant body temperature by panting. That's why when it's hot, they always have their tongues out...

Intelligence
Playfulness
Lovingness

Intelligence	4/4
Playfulness	4/4
Lovingness	4/4

NEWFOUNDLAND

Fluffy fur? Check! Massive body? Check! Sweet character? Check, check, check! The Newfoundland is one of the most popular breeds among families with children: these large dogs are extremely tame and protective of family members.

Strong and hardy, they live well indoors but need constant movement outdoors. They are also very skilled swimmers: when they see water they can hardly resist taking a dip!

Originally from the island of Newfoundland, Canada, these dogs used to help fishermen.

WOOF-WOW!

Some breeds—such as the golden retriever, Labrador retriever, and German shepherd—are, like the Newfoundland, skilled swimmers and are often employed as rescue dogs!

GOLDEN RETRIEVER

Intelligence
Playfulness
Lovingness

This medium-large dog is one of the sweetest and tame animals around, perfect for living with children. Be careful, however: it is so lively that it needs to move around constantly!

Best to have a large house and, if possible, also an outdoor space where it can run around. You also need to find the time to play with your friend and take frequent and eventful daily walks.

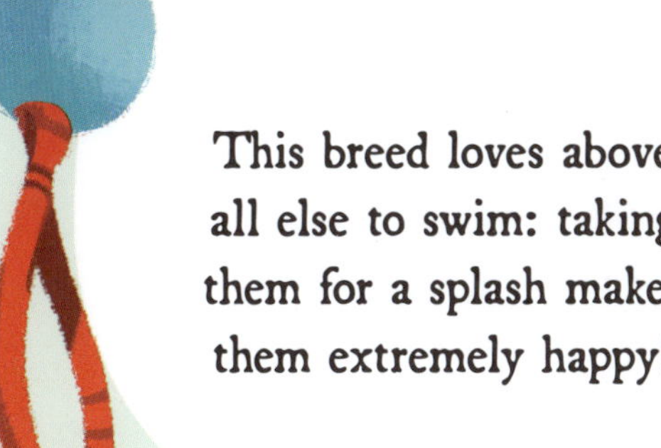

This breed loves above all else to swim: taking them for a splash makes them extremely happy!

DID YOU KNOW?

Dogs are able to sense human emotions. When a person is sad, for example, these dogs notice and come closer! That is why they are very often chosen as "emotional support animals," i.e., as help in cases of severe sadness.

HUSKY

Dogs of this breed have a muscular body and thick coat: this is because they come from the deep North of the world, where they were originally used to pull sleds in the snow. And they still do today in many countries, like Greenland!

They are not aggressive at all, but adopting one requires a lot of work because these dogs have strong personalities and are quite stubborn, less suited than others to living in a small home with a family.

Dogs of this breed may have eyes called heterochromatic: that is, of two different colors!

DID YOU KNOW?

To move their ears, dogs use about 18 different muscles! Not bad, uh?

Intelligence ✓✓✓✓

Playfulness ✓✓✓

Lovingness ✓✓✓

JACK RUSSELL TERRIER

This small dog is not to be underestimated! Members of this breed are real volcanoes, always on the move and ready to play!

They adapt well to apartment life, but that doesn't mean they don't need to let out all their urge to run. They were originally used in fox hunting, and their hunter instincts have never died down.

Highly intelligent animals that are well suited for training, Jack Russells are often featured in movies and TV series because they are well suited to the craft... of acting!

WOOF-WOW!

Dogs can understand up to 250 gestures and vocabulary that they are taught.

Intelligence
Playfulness
Lovingness

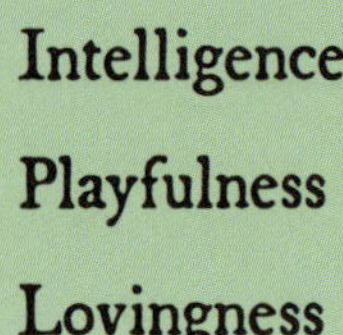

Intelligence
Playfulness
Lovingness

WELSH CORGI PEMBROKE

This funny and charming dog comes from Britain and has short legs, a long back, and big pointed ears! It was originally a herding dog, but now it is a perfect pet.

It is anything but lazy, though! It loves to play and move around a lot, so you have to be prepared to walk it often and engage it in entertaining games.

You have to be very careful about his diet so that he doesn't gain too much weight and can stay healthy for a long time!

WOOF-WOW!

Queen Elizabeth II of England loved this breed of dog very much and had several that accompanied her everywhere!

ENGLISH COCKER SPANIEL

The cocker spaniel, with its soft coat and long ears, is a sweet dog but also extremely determined! It needs to move every day, and for a long time: if you don't like outdoor walks and prefer to stay for hours on the couch with a good book, this is not the dog for you!

The cocker spaniel is a tame dog, but it has retained the hunting dog instincts it originally had, so perhaps it would not be safe for it to live with, for instance, a bunny...

Cocker spaniels can often be seen with funny earmuffs around their heads: these are used to prevent cold and dampness from causing diseases such as otitis, from which this breed particularly suffers.

DID YOU KNOW?

Dogs have a highly developed sense of smell compared to humans, while on the other hand their sense of taste is more limited: they have thousands fewer taste buds on their tongues!

Intelligence
Playfulness
Lovingness

GREYHOUND

Members of this breed are true athletes: greyhounds are incredible runners with lean bodies and sharp muzzles. They are also very sweet animals and perfect for family life.

They are shy with strangers and very quiet when indoors, but they need space in which to run safely and plenty of walks.

Greyhounds are an ancient breed: representations of them are even found in Egyptian art!

DID YOU KNOW?

When we cuddle our dog, the body secretes oxytocin, a mood-enhancing hormone. The animal secretes it, too, appreciating those moments!

Intelligence

Playfulness

Lovingness

Intelligence
Playfulness
Lovingness

ENGLISH BULLDOG

With its massive body and flattened muzzle, the English bulldog is unmistakable! Despite its heavy tonnage, it is a tame and docile animal, suitable for life with children.

It needs to move every day to stay fit, but you will probably have to convince it to do so by overcoming ts laziness and offering it short walks.

When the breed originated in medieval England, it was used to fight with bulls, as suggested by its name.

FRENCH BULLDOG

This small dog with a muscular and compact body has a characteristic flattened muzzle that gives it an adorable, somewhat rangy expression!

Its temperament is very sweet and affectionate, quiet, and suitable for living even in an apartment.

Intelligence
Playfulness
Lovingness

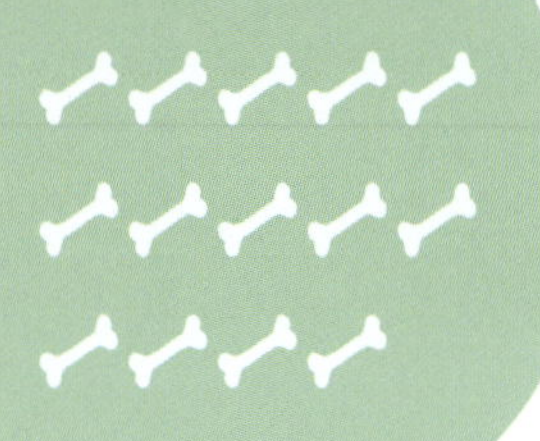

BORDER COLLIE

The border collie is an intelligent and energetic breed known for its incredible herding abilities. Often considered the smartest dog breed, border collies excel in obedience, agility, and problem-solving.

With their keen focus and tireless energy, they thrive in active environments and love having a job to do.

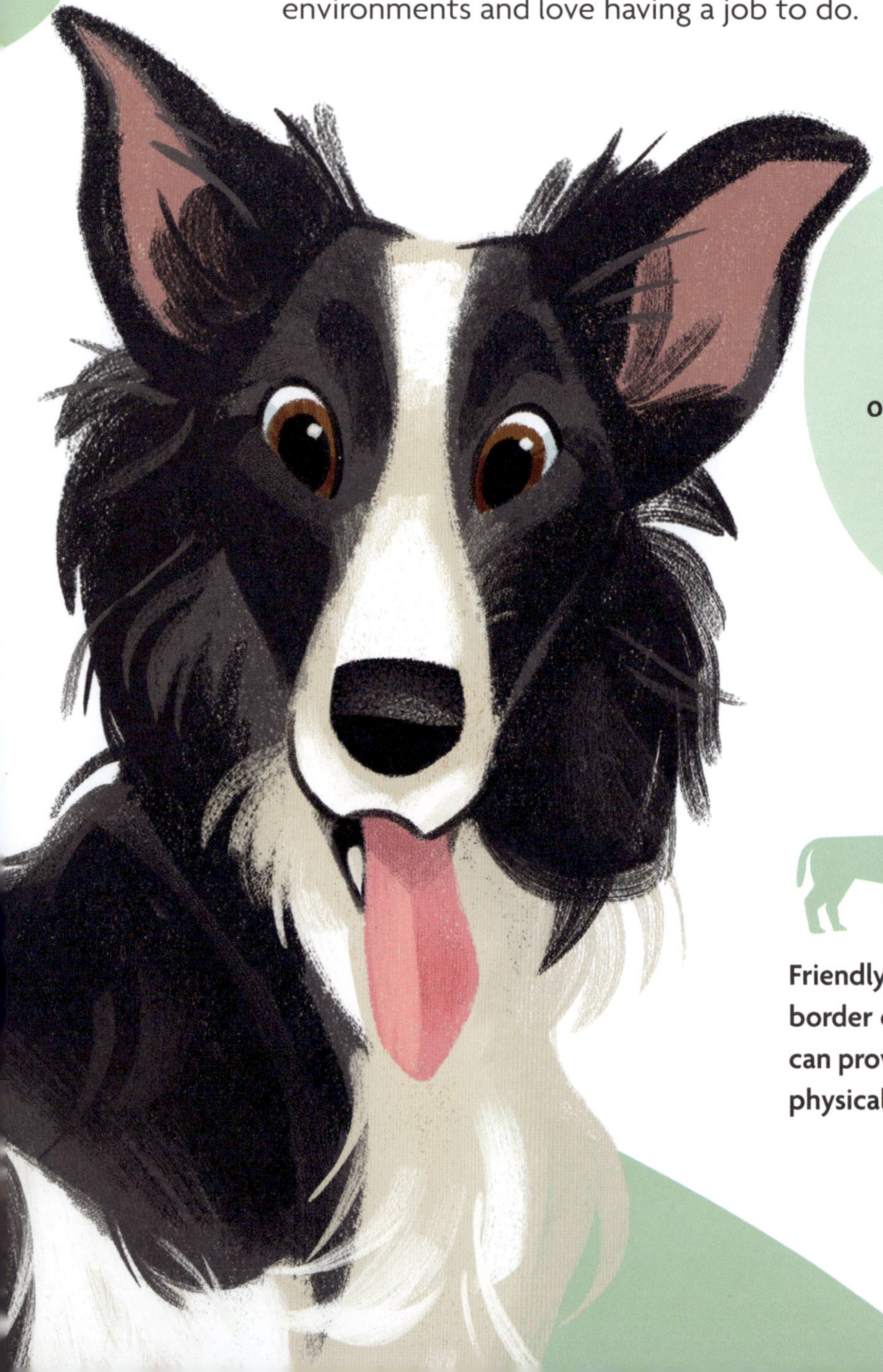

Their herding instincts are so strong that they often try to herd anything—people, cars, even other animals!

WOOF-WOW!

Friendly and affectionate with their families, border collies are best suited for owners who can provide them with plenty of mental and physical stimulation.

BASSET HOUND

The basset hound is a unique and charming breed known for its droopy ears, soulful eyes, and long, low body. Despite their slow, steady pace, these dogs are determined and persistent, which makes them excellent trackers.

Friendly and affectionate, basset hounds are great companions, although a bit stubborn.

Originally bred for hunting, basset hounds have an incredibly strong sense of smell, second only to the bloodhound.

DID YOU KNOW?

Dogs have an incredible sense of smell: a dog's sense of smell is 40 times more powerful than that of a human! This is why dogs are often used for search and rescue, as well as for detecting drugs, explosives, and even diseases like cancer.

Intelligence

Playfulness

Lovingness

POODLES

With their curly, soft fur, poodles are a real treat to pet! Dogs of this breed can be large, small, and...tiny! They are perfect animals for apartment life, sweet and affectionate with family members and strangers.

They also show great intelligence and can be trained to perform simple games—a perfect solution to let their incredible liveliness out!

Poodles don't lose their fur, which grows all the time!

DID YOU KNOW?

Dogs' ears are extraordinary: they can hear four times farther than human ears!

Intelligence
Playfulness
Lovingness

BEAGLE

Intelligence
Playfulness
Lovingness

Hey, do you hear that? Who is barking so much? Well yes, it is a beagle! The howl of these cute, medium-sized dogs is unique and unmistakable. They have a highly developed sense of smell, which is why in the past they were bred for hunting.

They are suitable for apartment life but their love of the outdoors has not abandoned them: they love long walks, to be taken, of course, with their noses to the ground!

One weakness of this breed? They are gluttonous! You have to be careful not to let them get overweight—they may have back problems!

WOOF-WOW!

How do dogs see? They are able to see not only black and white, but also the yellow and blue!

PAWS-ITIVELY PECULIAR PUPS

CHINESE CRESTED DOG

Those who want a truly curious-looking dog will be pleased with this breed. With its smooth body and head full of soft hair, these dogs are suitable for apartment life and are sweet and affectionate with family members. They do not like to be left alone, preferring to be taken everywhere by their human friends!

Intelligence
Playfulness
Lovingness

Intelligence
Playfulness
Lovingness

BEDLINGTON TERRIER

What does a Bedlington look like? Definitely a...white, curly sheep! Despite its cute appearance, however, this dog, in addition to being extremely lively and playful, has a courageous and determined character. In fact, its ancestors, originally from the United Kingdom, were used as hunting dogs...for mice! And they were also very skilled!

Intelligence
Playfulness
Lovingness

SHAR PEI

This breed originated in China, where it was used for fighting and hunting. Some trace of this origin has remained in the shar pei's temperament as it passionately protects its territory and its family, with whom it is affectionate and lovable. Its name, meaning "sand skin," perfectly describes the feeling one gets from stroking its adorable "wrinkles."

BERGAMASQUE SHEPHERD

A large dog, the Bergamasque shepherd has a very distinctive coat which forms hard weaves that give it a distinctive appearance. It is an animal that needs to move around a lot, so it is suitable for those with safe, outdoor spaces in which it can run. Like any dog originally used to control herds, it has a watchful, determined, and patient nature, but also a very strong personality that could require an equally assertive owner.

Intelligence
Playfulness
Lovingness

RODENTS

Tiny explorers with a knack for gnawing!

These small mammals are called rodents because, as the Latin word from which they derive their name suggests...they gnaw. And they do it all day long! That's right: teeth are very important for every species that is part of this family. Their teeth grow all the time, so they are always working hard to file them down with food, but also with wood or other small objects.

It is the responsibility of their owners to take care of this to keep the smiles on the little faces of their cute friends dazzling.

Intelligence
Playfulness
Lovingness

RABBIT

With soft fur and long ears, not to mention a fluffy tail, rabbits are very sweet animals that can live in apartments.

They must be provided with a large cage with special pellets, but they hate to be confined! They must be allowed to go outside and move freely. However, you have to be careful about what you leave around, because they gnaw everything!

Rabbits' teeth grow continuously, so they must always have hay or wood available to help them file them down.

INCREDIBLE PAWS!

Domestic rabbits come in many types: with tiny straight ears or long dangling ears, with short or long and very soft fur!

HAMSTER

Intelligence
Playfulness
Lovingness

Don't be fooled by its small size—the hamster is a very lively animal. In fact, it alternates between long sleeps and moments of great movement in its cage.

This is not an animal that can be left to roam around the house free, but it can be watched and handled with great care.

Hamsters are myopic! They do not see perfectly, but they rely on their sense of smell!

SUITABLE SPACE

Although it is a small rodent, it does not have to live in a tiny cage. It must have enough space to play and hide, and of course, a wheel to exercise on!

CHINCHILLA

With its rounded body and the sweetest look, the chinchilla is an irresistible animal, but adopters must be prepared to care for it.

You have to figure out whether or not it wants to be cuddled—some appreciate it, others don't! And it does not live happily with other pets, such as dogs and cats.

These rodents love to take baths—sand baths! You can find very fine sand on the market with which to fill containers that they use to clean their fur by rolling around!

PLANED CAGE

This animal needs a large cage with a dark, sheltered area and multiple floors for climbing and playing.

Intelligence
Playfulness
Lovingness

GUINEA PIG

Small and very shy rodents, guinea pigs can live in apartments either in large, equipped cages or left free in secure environments. They should be handled very gently, fed properly, and cleaned daily.

They communicate with friendly vocalizations and do not get along too well with other animals such as dogs and cats.

These animals are able to sleep with their eyes open, since they are preyed upon in the wild.

POPPING

When excited and happy, these pets do jumps and prances that are called "popping," like popcorn when it pops!

Intelligence
Playfulness
Lovingness

Intelligence	4/5
Playfulness	3/5
Lovingness	3/5

MOUSE

Most people try very hard to get rid of them, but mice can be adopted as pets! You can find them in animal shelters, and it is best to have two or three of them to keep each other company—of the same gender, otherwise there will be babies!

The cage should be large and on several levels, and when mice are awake they need to play a lot!

If habituated, mice are not afraid of being touched by humans. In fact, they are real cuddle champions!

MICE OR RAT?

The difference is in size: mice are smaller than rats, but both can live with humans.

SQUIRREL

Although they are a symbol of wildlife, squirrels can also be adopted as pets. Not all, however, are well adapted to captivity. They are not easy pets to house: they need a lot of freedom, especially vertically!

So you have to equip yourself with an aviary and have a garden, because squirrels would suffer indoors!

Squirrels are extremely territorial animals: avoid adopting more than one!

BEWARE OF THE LAW

Not all species of squirrels are allowed by law: in addition to considering the welfare of the small rodent, you should inform yourself before considering adopting one!

Intelligence
Playfulness
Lovingness

HEDGEHOG

Small and covered with quills, hedgehogs are very tame animals that can become pets according to the law of the country where you live (so you should always check first!).

To take them in, you need to ensure an environment with the right temperature—between 25 and 27 degrees Celsius—and small shelters in which they can hide. Hedgehogs are indeed very shy and are frightened by sudden loud noises.

Hedgehogs are insectivorous mammals, so their food will consist of crickets and moths, as well as fresh fruits and vegetables!

QUILLING

In the first few months of life, hedgehogs lose many quills, so-called "quilling," to make room for others to grow in their place.

Intelligence

Playfulness

Lovingness

GERBIL

Intelligence
Playfulness
Lovingness

This tiny rodent comes from arid savannah areas and has become a popular pet.

Sweet and tame, it lives well if placed in a large cage with soil and multiple levels to move around. It must be handled with great care and without lifting it, especially by its tail!

When frightened, the gerbil beats its paws vigorously on the ground as a warning to its peers.

S.O.S. FRIENDS

The gerbil is an animal that suffers extremely from loneliness: you should consider adopting more than one!

FINS, SCALES, AND FEATHERS

Let's talk about birds, fish, reptiles, and amphibians...

Which of them fascinates you the most? They are all really different from each other but have one thing in common: they can be adopted to live at home with us! Each of them needs to be treated with all consideration, respecting their characteristics. Some don't like to be touched, while others like it.

It is always good to get the best information before choosing!

Intelligence ●●
Playfulness ●
Lovingness ●

GOLDFISH

It lives in freshwater, and watching it swim is really relaxing! Even if it is just a little fish, it must have a suitable aquarium and not a small glass bowl! The temperature then must be between 12 and 23 degrees Celsius, and filters must be used to ensure the quality of the liquid in which the fish lives.

A fairly simple pet to adopt, in short, but one that requires a little preparation and a lot of care!

WATER TEST

Before you immerse your fish in the aquarium, test the composition of the water with special strips to check that it does not contain excessive amounts of substances that could harm it, such as ammonia.

WATER TURTLE

These small reptiles with a proud expression live between water and land. Very small turtles can be found, but some can grow to over 30 centimeters in diameter!

They should not live in tiny containers, but in suitable aquariums—called aquaterrariums—where they can have dry areas and plenty of water to splash around in!

BASKING LAMPS

Water turtles benefit from having a special lamp that illuminates an area of the terrarium where they can "sunbathe" and absorb heat and UV rays.

Intelligence ●●●
Playfulness ●
Lovingness ●

Intelligence ●●●
Playfulness ●
Lovingness ●

FIGHTING FISH

Originally from Asia, this small freshwater fish with fins that seem to "flutter" in the water has a very special feature: the males of the species fight each other!

This is why you should not keep more than one in an aquarium, better to have several females, with only one male.

GROUND TURTLE

A ground turtle can also be raised outside in a protected area of the garden—so it is perfect for those who have one! For turtles not to escape, an enclosure must be built that extends both in height and underground—they are in fact skilled diggers!—and that is lit by the sun.

They must then always have clean water and grass available.

Intelligence ●●●
Playfulness ●
Lovingness ●

Intelligence ●●●●
Playfulness ●
Lovingness ●

IGUANA

This magnificent reptile is much loved as a pet, but it is not at all easy to raise!

For one thing, it grows a lot and can measure up to one meter in length! That's why it needs a large terrarium with a branch for climbing. And its temperament can turn out to be "wild," especially in male specimens.

Iguanas need to live in moist, warm environments—with special UV lamps for them to warm up—and particular soil that must be cleaned daily.

ESCAPE ROOM

Lively iguanas often try to escape from the terrarium. Unfortunately, our homes offer them many dangers; it is best to avoid pandering to its escapes!

CRESTED GECKO

Intelligence ●●●
Playfulness ●
Lovingness ●●

Among reptiles to raise indoors, the crested gecko is among those that are best suited even for the inexperienced. Its terrarium is not too large, and it does not need UV lamps because it is a nocturnal animal, but a dense environment of plants should be recreated.

In addition, the average temperature of a house is fine for it, and it feeds on insects and fruit.

Tamer than other reptiles, it needs to be handled with extreme care because it tends to pounce out of your hands!

INDOOR CLIMBING

Crested geckos love to climb, so you must equip the terrarium with a vertical surface made of abrasive material on which they can have fun!

Intelligence ●●●
Playfulness ●●
Lovingness ●●●

PARROT

Colorful and talkative, the parrot is really an amazing bird! It can also be raised as a pet, but with great care!

This bird is not small in size, so its cage will have to be very large and vertical.

A PLAYROOM FOR PLAYFUL BIRDS

Parrots are very lively and playful animals: they must therefore have plenty of toys and pastimes made especially for them.

CANARY

This tiny, colorful songbird has been domesticated since the 1500s! Naturally wary of humans, it must be approached without abrupt movements and not be startled with loud noises, screams, or sudden shaking of its cage.

Otherwise, it may become sick from the stress coming from the surroundings!

Intelligence ●●●
Playfulness ●●
Lovingness ●●●

PARAKEET

The little parakeet has a sociable nature and is very curious. Some breeds are so intelligent that they are able to learn simple games and tricks and imitate the sound of other animals' cries or even some human words!

In short, it will be the perfect companion for those who are looking for a definitely chatty friend!

The most popular domestic parakeets are the collared parakeets from Australia.

FRIENDS WANTED

Parakeets are sociable animals, so it would be best not to keep them alone but at least in pairs!

Intelligence

Playfulness

Lovingness

RIENDS FROM ALL OVER THE WORLD!

Out of the ordinary pets!

Have you ever thought about having an insect as a pet? Or a sheep? Maybe it sounds crazy to you, but there are places in the world where it's perfectly normal! Browse the next few pages to discover some of the most bizarre and strange pets on the planet. How many of them have you seen in person?

Would you like to have one of your own, or would you prefer a cat, dog, or goldfish?

HOUSE CRICKET

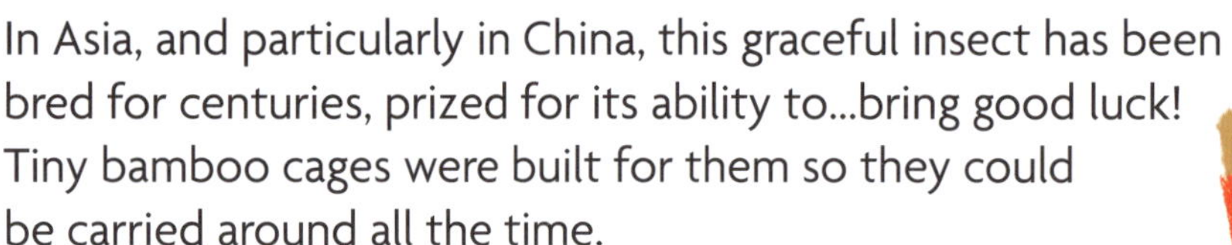

In Asia, and particularly in China, this graceful insect has been bred for centuries, prized for its ability to...bring good luck! Tiny bamboo cages were built for them so they could be carried around all the time.

Today, they have to be kept in special cases with a constant temperature for you to have the pleasure of observing them for a few weeks: their average life span is unfortunately around only two or three months!

In ancient times, even Chinese emperors owned pet crickets!

SPECIAL FOOD

Is there such a thing as cricket food, just like dog food or cat food? Well, yes! You can find it in specialized stores and combine it with vegetables, fruits, some grains, and even... dead insects like flies and mosquitoes!

Intelligence ★
Playfulness ★
Lovingness ★

HAWK

Intelligence ★★★★
Playfulness ★
Lovingness ★

Even thousands of years ago, this magnificent bird of prey accompanied humans during hunting, giving rise to a version of it called "falconry." Today, hawks are still bred—but not kept indoors!—and trained. They are most beloved in the Middle East.

They are difficult birds to keep as pets, and to do so you have to know them very well!

The hawk is the national bird of Qatar! In Abu Dhabi, UAE, a clinic has been established to care for hawks, the first in the world.

SPECIAL HOOD

Hawks are wild animals, unaccustomed to contact with humans. To help tame them, a special hood is used that temporarily deprives them of sight so they can gradually adapt to the environment.

Intelligence ★★★
Playfulness ★★★
Lovingness ★★★★

SUGAR GLIDER

This tiny marsupial comes from the forests of Australia and Tasmania. It is a very sweet little animal, just like the fruit and sap it loves to feed on and that earned it its curious name.

Before adopting one, you need to be sure that you have a suitable home for it: it cannot stay in a small cage and must have a tall aviary available so that it can launch itself into the air.

Thanks to special membranes that resemble "wings," sugar gliders can take leaps of up to 50 meters in length. If left loose in the house, they climb and launch from place to place, so any hazards such as open windows should be avoided.

SOCIAL ANIMAL

Sugar gliders love to be in groups: for this reason, it is best to adopt at least two of them so that they do not suffer from loneliness!

SHEEP

Intelligence ★★★

Playfulness ★★★

Lovingness ★★★

We are used to seeing them grazing in flocks, but in some parts of the world, such as Senegal, sheep are considered pets!

To keep them close to you, however, you must have a large, open space in which to build a sheltered area, with hay always available and clean water. Also, a sheep should not be left alone: it is a social animal!

Sheep are very intelligent animals that can be trained to learn simple games.

WHICH BREED?

There are about 200 breeds of sheep, varying in size and needs, and to keep one as a pet you should choose the one that best suits your environment.

Intelligence ★★★
Playfulness ★★
Lovingness ★★

ALPACA

In Peru, alpacas are not only animals to breed for their very fine wool, but also real pets! Beware, however, that they cannot be kept indoors: they must have a clean barn in which to shelter and plenty of green space in which to walk and graze the grass on which they feed.

Also, alpacas live in flocks, so they need to live in groups made up of many animals and not alone. In short, I think you will have to give up the dream of housing an alpaca in your bedroom...

It is often confused with its larger "cousin," the llama!

NO SPITTING

When they feel in danger, alpacas may spit. They rarely do so toward humans, however; it is more common to happen between animals of the same species.

VIETNAMESE DWARF PIGLET

This sweet pig can be adopted for domestic life, although in adulthood it can reach a considerable weight! It has long been a pet in Canada and the United States.

It cannot live indoors, but must have a protected place outside at its disposal, with the ability to move freely and explore the environment.

Despite the reputation of being an animal with little interest in hygiene, this breed is actually very clean.

GUARD HOGS

These animals are very territorial; when strangers enter the space they consider to be theirs, they may engage in aggressive behaviors just like guard dogs.

Intelligence ★★★
Playfulness ★★★
Lovingness ★★★

PRAIRIE DOG

They are called "dogs," but, in fact, they are friendly rodents native to the American Great Plains. It was there that they began to be bred as pets, revealing a sweet and tame nature, and they are very affectionate with humans!

They must be kept in a protected outdoor area and adopted in multiples because they suffer greatly from loneliness.

CLEANING

Prairie dogs can be trained to use a litter box for their needs, like cats!

When they meet, these animals recognize each other by touching each other's noses, as if it were a greeting!

Intelligence ★★★
Playfulness ★★★
Lovingness ★★★

STAG BEETLE

Intelligence ★★★
Playfulness ★
Lovingness ★

In Japan, pets are beloved: dogs, cats, rabbits, and...insects! That's right: especially in the countryside, children like to keep certain kinds of insects as friends, and the most popular is the stag beetle.

It is a large beetle—almost 9 centimeters long!—that displays what appear to be large antlers, but they are actually its mandibles! It is a harmless and peaceful insect and is winged, so it can fly among the plants it feeds on.

When it is a larva, the stag beetle can live up to 10 years. When it becomes an adult, however, its life expectancy is only a few weeks!

WHAT LUCK!

In many cultures, spotting a stag beetle is a lucky sign!

Intelligence
Playfulness
Lovingness

DWARF GOAT

Native to Senegal, this small goat is an animal that can be raised if you have an adequate fenced outdoor space that can also contain a small house in which to shelter and...other goats!

That's right: goats do not like to be alone, so it would be best to adopt at least two!

SO MUCH CHATTER!

Dwarf goats communicate through their bleats—this way you can tell when they are hungry, thirsty, or afraid!

Apparently, dwarf goats seem to recognize the humans they live with and react by showing great excitement!

DWARF ROYAL PYTHON

Intelligence ★★
Playfulness ★
Lovingness ★

It may seem crazy to keep a large snake in the house, but this species is particularly quiet. This is not to say that adopting one as a pet will prove easy—it is definitely a reptile for experts!

The dwarf python needs a large terrarium with hiding places and a container with moist moss that resembles its natural habitat, as well as a climate with temperatures that vary from day to night.

Pythons are not venomous, as they crush prey with their mighty bodies. When handling them, however, it is necessary to be very careful. If frightened, they may bite!

MIMETIC BODY

The dwarf royal python has a very distinctive colored skin: it serves, in the wild, to blend in with its environment and better attack prey.

FENNEC

This fox lives in the North African desert, and in some countries of the world, such as Japan, it is considered a pet. In many others, however, it is illegal to adopt one!

The fennec is wild and adapts with much difficulty to life away from nature, and it may show restless behavior. It is also likely to suffer in climates other than that of its native desert.

The fennec is covered with thin and very dense fur, even under its paws: this enables it to walk even on the scorching sand of the desert.

WHAT EARS!

The fennec has very large and pointed ears. Why are they so developed? Because they allow it to sense every movement of the small insects and small animals it feeds on, even in the middle of the sand.

Intelligence ★★★

Playfulness ★

Lovingness ★

AXOLOTL

Intelligence ★
Playfulness ★
Lovingness ★

This friendly aquatic salamander is native to Mexico, where it was considered a sacred animal by the ancient Aztecs. It has a very distinctive appearance and is found in a range of colors—about 20!—ranging from black to very light pink, almost transparent!

Its aquarium requires a constant water temperature, with no surges, which can be lethal to the animal!

Axolotls are able to regrow a limb when amputated by an accident and also internal organs, up to five times!

DON'T TOUCH

Axolotls, like aquarium fish, should not be handled unless absolutely necessary.

Intelligence ★
Playfulness ★
Lovingness ★

STICK INSECT

This unusual insect can be raised indoors, so you can observe it every day as it perfectly blends in with the environment!

To allow it to live at its best, it is necessary to prepare a large terrarium filled with branches of the plants it feeds on, so that in addition to eating it can climb and live among the leaves. To moisturize it, water should be sprayed into the terrarium once or twice a week.

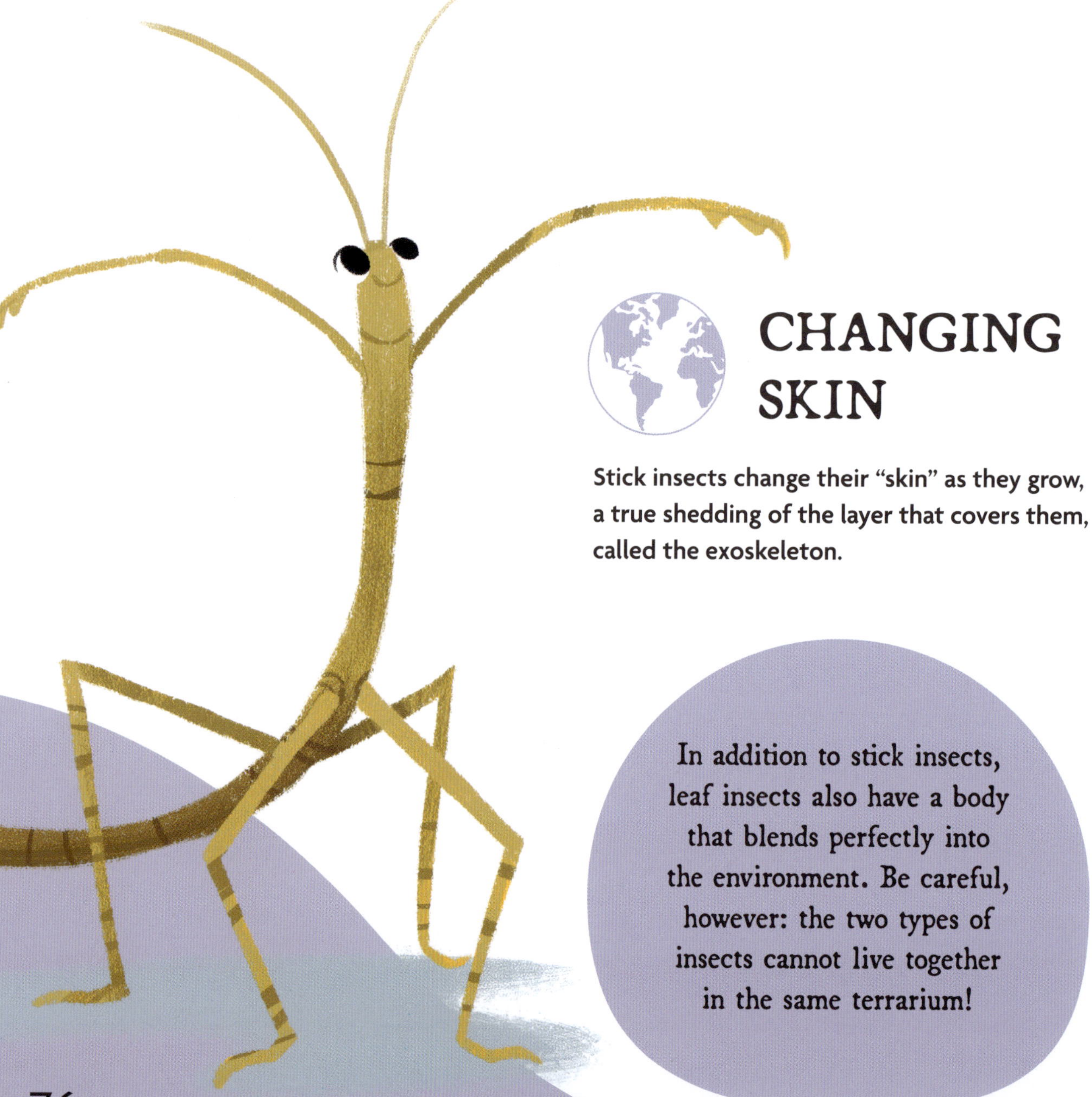

CHANGING SKIN

Stick insects change their "skin" as they grow, a true shedding of the layer that covers them, called the exoskeleton.

In addition to stick insects, leaf insects also have a body that blends perfectly into the environment. Be careful, however: the two types of insects cannot live together in the same terrarium!

LEMUR

Intelligence ★★
Playfulness ★★
Lovingness ★

This two-colored tailed monkey is native to the island of Madagascar and is sometimes chosen as a pet, even though it is illegal to adopt one in many countries!

As is always the case with wild animals that are bred indoors, it is very difficult to tame them completely, and they may suffer greatly from being away from their peers and their natural habitat.

Observing the way these animals interact in the wild, ethologists have noticed that each individual shows a particular character: some remain aloof and prefer to be alone, and some like group life.

SMELLY FIGHTING

Lemurs have glands on their wrists and chest that secrete odorous substances to mark territory, and when they fight with each other, they also use these strong odors.

WHAT IS THE PERFECT PET FOR YOU?

Answer the questions, then count how many times you chose each letter. The one you marked the most matches the best choice!

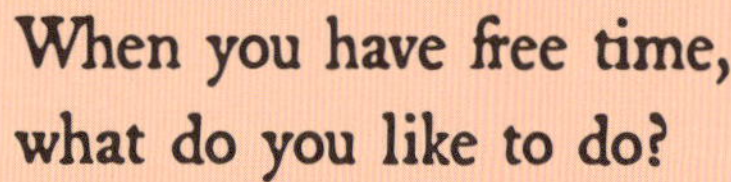

When you have free time, what do you like to do?

A- Run to the park and play ball

B- Sofa and television

C- A swim in the pool

D- Sleep

How would you define yourself? Choose from the adjectives:

A- Lively

B- Independent

C- Rare

D- Sleepy

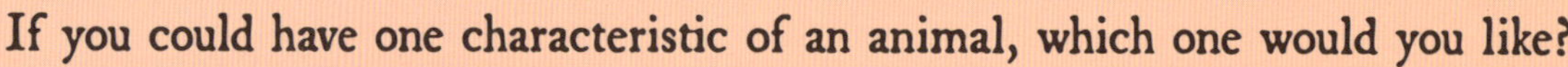

If you could have one characteristic of an animal, which one would you like?

A- Run very fast

B- Be able to make long jumps

C- Fly

D- Be able to bite any material

Majority of responses A

Your ideal pet is a DOG! Loyal, affectionate, dynamic—it depends on the breed!—and eager to spend time with you.

Majority of responses B

Independent, mysterious, and charming, the CAT is perfect for you! You can play with him when he feels like it, and enjoy his purrs and cuddles.

How would you define your home?
A- A place to defend
B- A place to sleep
C- A place to live
D- A place to shelter

Ideal vacation:
A- Hiking in the mountains
B- I'd rather stay at home
C- In the air for a magnificent trip
D- In the countryside, relaxing

What do you think about sports?
A- I love them
B- Only when I feel like it
C- Why not?
D- Better to take a nap

Your favorite snack:
A- Ham sandwich
B- Ice cream
C- Fresh fruit
D- Peanuts

Majority of responses C

From a two- or four-legged friend you don't want forced direct contact, but you're content to observe and care for him! So even a FISH, a TURTLE, or a BIRD is fine!

Majority of responses D

You won't be able to resist having a sweet BUNNY, HAMSTER, or MOUSE to take care of! You can watch as they play, eat, and sleep in their burrows.

Rachel Foo
is a Malaysian illustrator from a city famous for its bean sprouts. She graduated with honors in Illustration from Curtin University in Australia and worked as a concept artist and visual developer in independent game design studios in Melbourne. After returning to Malaysia, she dedicated herself to illustration full-time, drawing inspiration from nature and the beauty in small things. In her free time, she enjoys hiking in the rainforest, urban skating, and sharing her passion for art with children.

Altea Villa
has a doctor of modern history degree in social history. Since 2018, she has been a content writer for children's magazines and books, particularly focused on divulgation and "edutainment."

Piazzale Luigi Cadorna, 6
20123 Milan, Italy
www.whitestar.it

Editing: Abby Young

First printing, April 2026

ISBN 978-88-544-2194-3
1 2 3 4 5 6   30 29 28 27 26

Printed and manufactured in China by
Allied Fortune Times Limited (AF printing)
Dongguan City, Guangdong Province, P.R. China